THE SENIOR DUMMIES' GUIDE TO THE TOP 5 ANDROID USABILITY TIPS

How to Set Up Your Android Device For Easy Use

By Kevin Brandt

Edited by Gene Lass

ISBN-13: 978-1979045599

ISBN-10: 1979045593

1st Edition

You Are Not A Dummy!

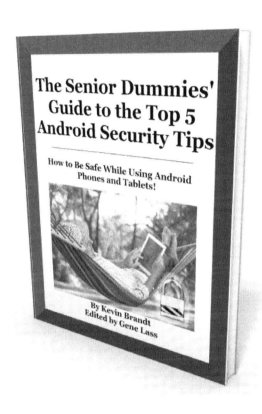

More is waiting for you with the Senior Dummies' newsletter! Hear about upcoming releases, more tips and information to share with your friends. Become the tech-savvy senior that you always knew you could be! If you have already signed up for the newsletter (and got this as a free e-book) then thank you! To sign up for the newsletter, tap or click below (on an e-book reader device) or browse to:

Go to: http://www.seniordummies.com/free-gift

Other books are available or coming soon, including:

The Senior Dummies' Guide to iPhone and iPad Tips and Tricks
The Senior Dummies' Guide to the Top 5 Android Security Tips
The Senior Dummies' Guide to Android Tips and Tricks

Find them on Amazon.com!

About Kevin Brandt...

Author Kevin Brandt has over 20 years of professional technology experience in software development and teaching on a host of platforms. Making new technology easy to use for everyone is a passion of his.

Blog: www.kevinbrandt.com
Twitter: @kevindbrandt

About Gene Lass...

Gene Lass is a writer and editor with more than 20 years of experience. He has worked in all forms of printed media, from books to blogs, on a wide variety of topics. He most frequently writes about health care, finance, technology, and pop culture. Contact him at genelass2@juno.com.

Contents

Chapter 1
Introduction

"The way to get started is to quit talking and begin doing."

– Walt Disney, Animator

Let me tell you a story. I know a senior who had a flip cell phone for the longest time. He really loved it and enjoyed its similarity to standard land line phones. Then, one day, the phone just stopped working. Completely. Nothing worked to bring it back from the dead. He had heard much about the new smartphones on the market and so he bought one. This is where the trouble started. He came to me, very worried, and said, "I don't understand how I can get this new phone to work for me! I can't hear it sometimes and I can't see the letters on he screen. Help!" After calming him down and showing him a few tips, I decided to write this free guide.

If you bought an Android-based device and want to learn a few tips on making it easier for you to work with, this is the book for you!

Within these pages, you'll find the tips that will enable your new device to work the way you want it to work.

These tips are designed for you, the senior Android user; to focus on the tips you probably want to know the most. Before you plunge in, though, here are some basic rules and reminders:

- This book assumes basic computer and technology knowledge. This is not a total beginner's guide, so if you have never touched a computer, you may need to start with more basic information.

- The pictures of the screenshots you see here may not be exactly what you might see on your screen because Android has a wide variety of "skins" (basically different screen images, colors and sizes). However, the icons and images tend to be close, so use a little instinct and try some things out if you don't see an exact match.

- Some of the screenshots will have portions blurred out to protect the innocent...or at least the anonymity of the kind contributors who took the screenshots in the first place. No need to worry about that, the information underneath the blur will be different than yours so just go with whatever you see on your screen.

- On the screenshots you'll see white circles. These indicate places on the screen to touch with your finger. The circles have been added to guide you, but you won't actually see them on your screen.

- You may notice that some screens shown are larger or smaller than others. That's because some have been taken from a tablet (larger) and some pictures have been taken from a smartphone (smaller).

- The term "device" here is used to take the place of saying "phone or tablet" all the time.

- Above all, rule #1 really is: DO NOT PANIC! (The book was almost titled that, by the way). You're not likely to really mess anything up. So, go ahead and try out these tips for yourself.

Finally, you don't have to read the book cover to cover. Jump around to the different sections of the book and check out the tips you think may be most useful to you. Enjoy your new device!

Chapter 2
See Me, Feel Me

"It is during our darkest moments that we must focus to see the light."

– Aristotle, Philosopher

The sad truth is that as we age, we may need some help with seeing things without greater effort than before. Until medical science comes up with a full cure for vision loss, we may need our "readers" right? These tips are designed to help all of us with some trouble focusing on the screen of our devices.

o. Opening Your Device Settings

This is a key tip that you will use over and over again with your device, so it's tip number zero. To change anything you want, you will need to get to the Settings menus.

Step 1: Put your finger on the little images on the upper right of the screen. ↓

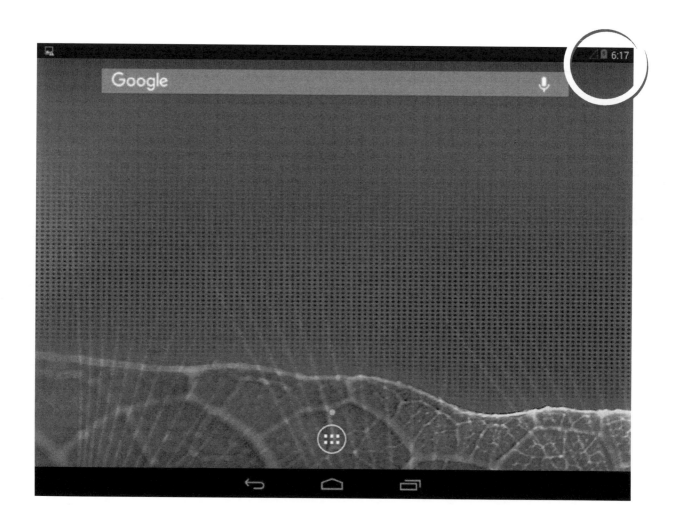

Step 2: Swipe down (hold your finger on the screen and drag it down). ↓

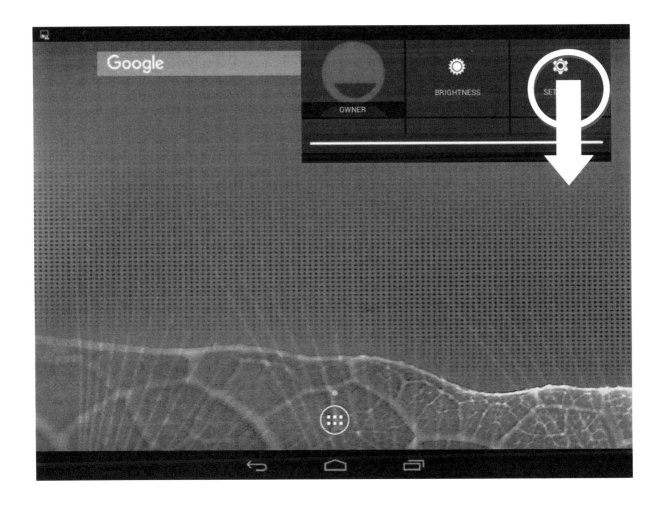

Step 3: Now with the menu fully displayed you can tap the Settings button. ↓

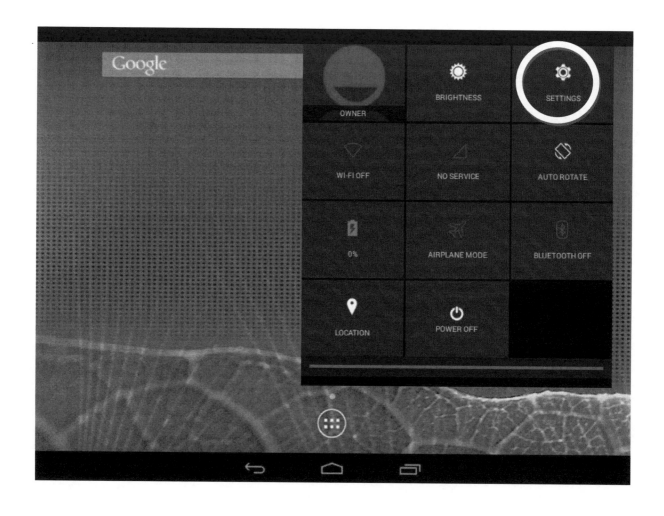

1. Time for Large Text

There are times when you just want to be able to read the screen without squinting or using glasses (Is there anyone out there who loves their "readers"...No? I didn't think so). It's simple to set all the text on the device to a large (or huge) size.

Step 1: Go to Settings. ↓

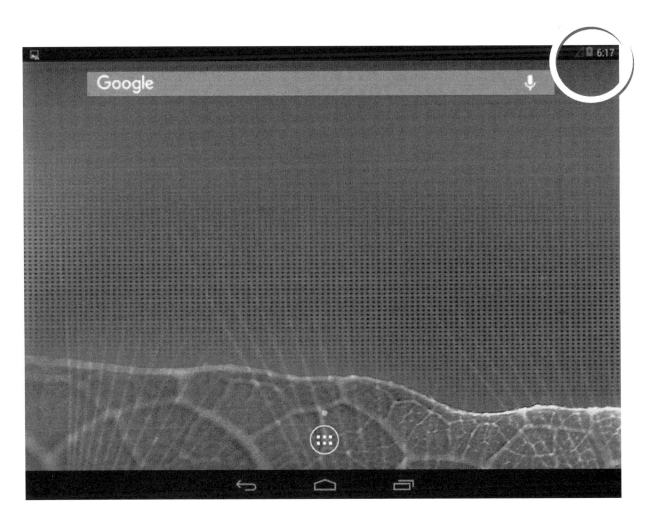

Step 2: Tap Display. ↓

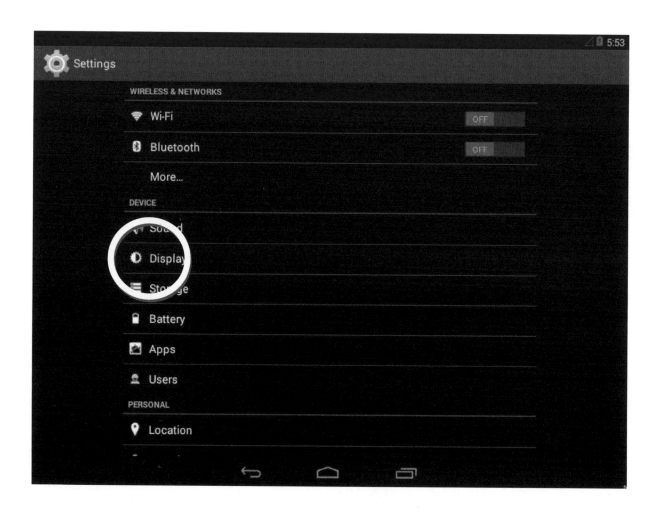

Step 3: Tap Font Size. ↓

Step 4: Select the right font size for you! ↓

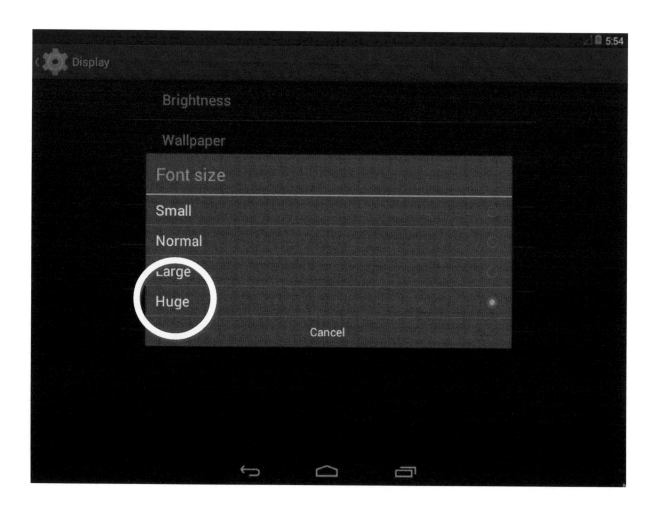

2. Change Your Background

If you want the normal background (also known as wallpaper) that you see to be something different, there are a few easy steps to take. Maybe you want a picture of loved ones, that vacation you took, or a picture of your garden. It's quick and easy to change the existing background to any image you have on the device or to change it to one of the standard ones that come with Android. There are even animated backgrounds!

One word of caution: Some of the backgrounds can really use quite a bit of your device's battery power and speed. So, you may not want to use the animated backgrounds if you want your battery to last a long time.

Step 1: Go to Settings. ↓

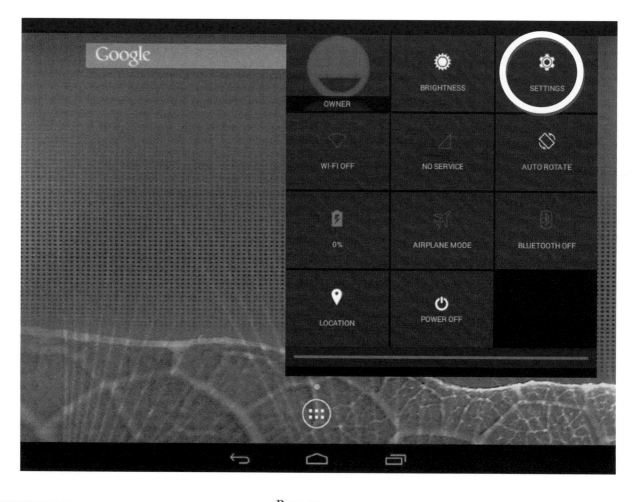

Step 2: Tap Display. ↓

Step 3: Tap Wallpaper. ↓

Step 4: Select Gallery, Live Wallpapers, Photos or Wallpapers. Gallery and Photos allow you to pick an image from the pictures on your device...perhaps that nice one of the grandchildren? Live Wallpapers gives you the ones that are animated and Wallpapers are ones built in that don't move. All you need to do is tap the one that you like and it will become your background.

3. Turn on Talkback via the Accessibility Options

The Accessibility settings area is a great resource to help you get the most out of your device. It's amazing what additional features are buried in there to help with making the screen easier to read and your device easier to use. Some of these are so useful that I recommend them for anyone, not just someone with, perhaps, vision problems.

Talkback is an absolutely unbelievable feature that most people don't know about. It can provide spoken information about what you touch, select or activate. Here's how to turn it on.

Step 1: Go to Settings. ↓

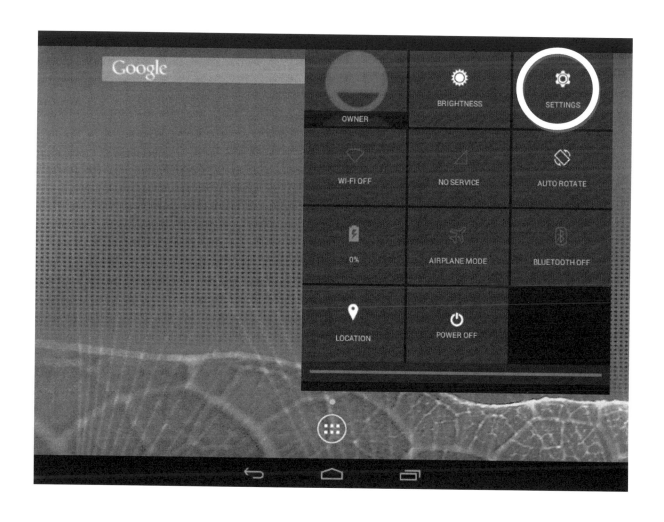

Step 2: Go to Accessibility. ↓

Step 3: Tap the Talkback setting. ↓

Step 4: Swipe the Off button to On. The device will then start up a series of lessons on how to use that feature (not shown here). Make sure your volume is high enough for you to hear the (slightly computerized) voice tell you how it works. Enjoy! ↓

Magnify with Just a Flick

So, the images on the screen are still not big enough? No problem! Here is the tip for you!

Step 1: Go to Settings. ↓

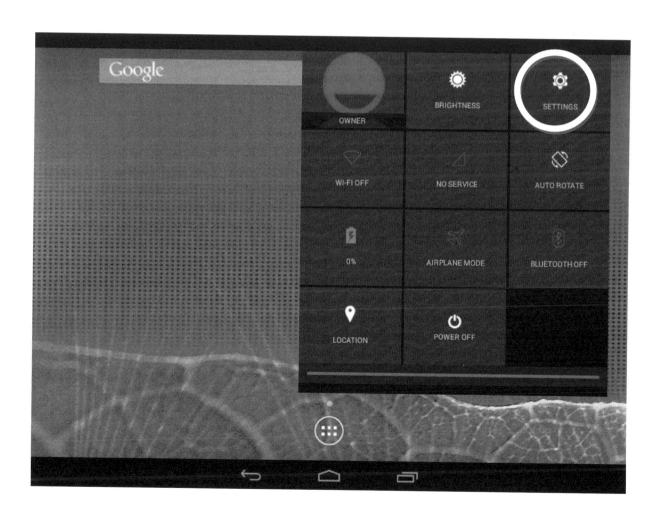

Step 2: Tap the Accessibility option. ↓

Step 3: Tap the Magnification gestures option. ↓

Step 4: Read the description on how to use it and Swipe the Off button to On. Generally, a triple tap magnifies the portion of the screen you want to see close up. ↓

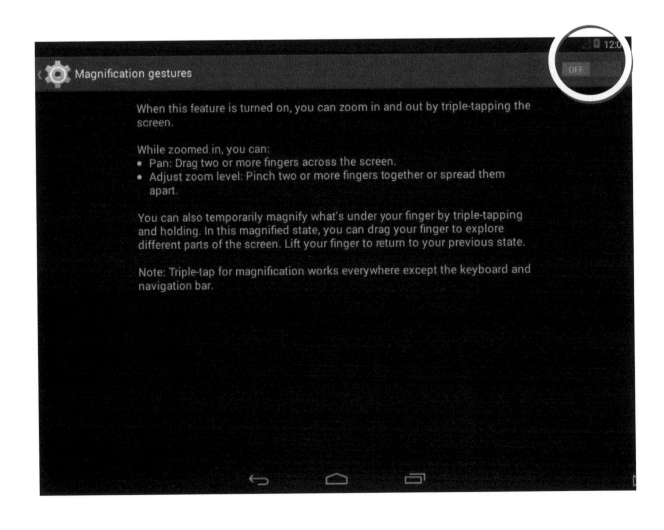

Chapter 3
Hear Me!

"Freedom is the right to tell people what they do not want to hear."

– George Orwell, Author

If you are checking out this last tip, you may be like me. I suffered some hearing loss in my youth that never bothered me until my later years. I began to realize that it certainly would be nice to use my device but not have to worry about being able to hear it when it made sounds.

This tip can help you overcome any hearing loss like mine. It is handy to use and easy to turn on. Read on for a simple way your device can help you out.

5. Enable Captions

For folks who may not be able to hear the device in a very noisy environment or any environment, captions can be a great help. It basically displays closed captioning, much like a TV.

Step 1: Get to Settings. ↓

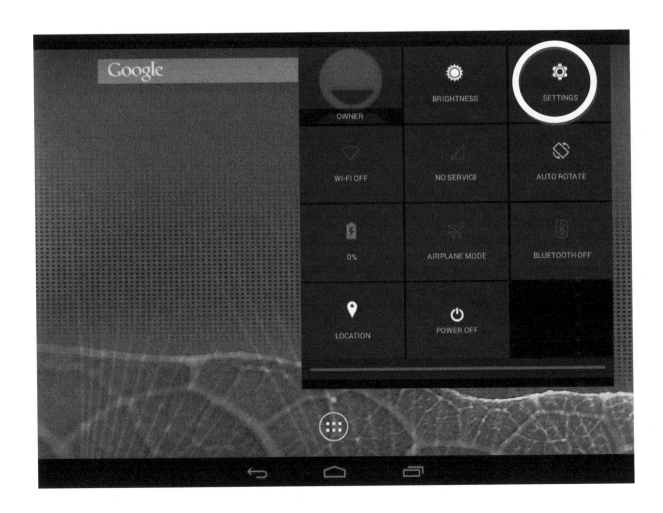

Step 2: Then tap Accessibility. ↓

Step 3: Tap the Captions option. ↓

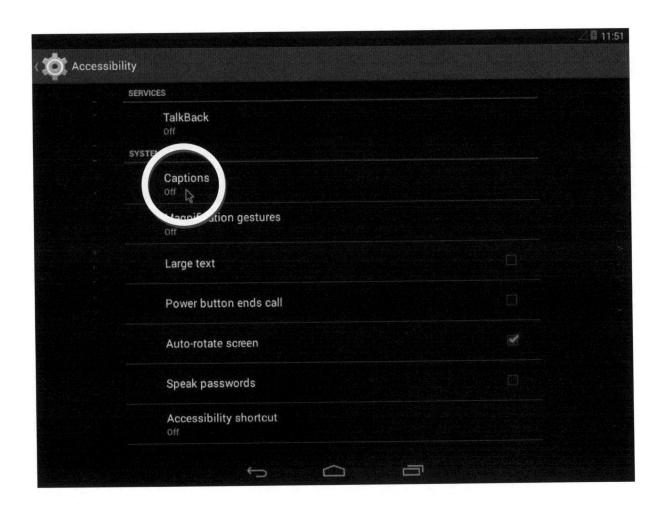

Step 3: Swipe the Off button to On. ↓

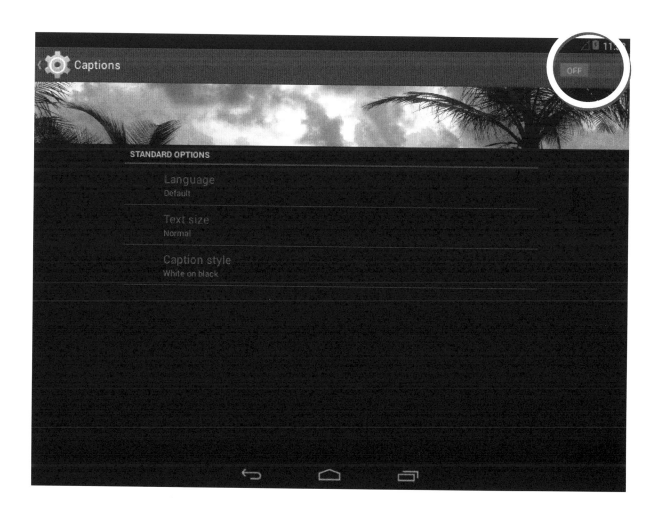

The rest of the options just change the way the caption is shown on the screen. You can experiment with these until you get the text exactly how you want it to look.

Chapter 4
Thank You!

"I can no other answer make, but, thanks, and thanks."

– William Shakespeare, Playwright

Thank you for reading this free book! If you got it from a friend, thank them! With this information, I hope you are well on your way to feeling more secure with your device.

If you haven't already done so (maybe you got this FREE e-book from a friend), go to the Senior Dummies' website and take a look. You can even sign up for the Senior Dummies' email newsletter. Occasionally but not too often you will receive an email with more tips, information about other useful products and news of upcoming releases.

http://www.seniordummies.com

Enjoy and thank you!

You Are Not A Dummy!

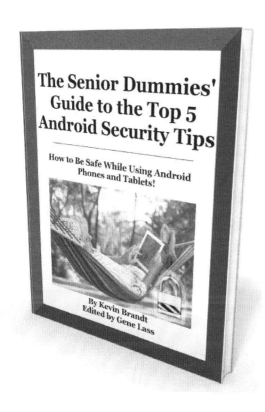

More is waiting for you with the Senior Dummies' newsletter! Hear about upcoming releases, more tips and information to share with your friends. Become the tech-savvy senior that you always knew you could be! If you have already signed up for the newsletter (and got this as a free e-book) then thank you! To sign up for the newsletter, tap or click below (on an e-book reader device) or browse to:

Go to: http://www.seniordummies.com/free-gift

Other books are available or coming soon, including:

The Senior Dummies' Guide to iPhone and iPad Tips and Tricks
The Senior Dummies' Guide to the Top 5 Android Security Tips
The Senior Dummies' Guide to Android Tips and Tricks

Find them on Amazon.com!

Printed in Great Britain
by Amazon